The A to Z
Beastly Jamboree

The A to Z
Beastly Jamboree

Robert Bender

DUTTON   Lodestar Books   NEW YORK

Library of Congress Cataloging-in-Publication Data
Bender, Robert.
The A to Z beastly jamboree / Robert Bender.—1st ed.
p.   cm.
ISBN 0-525-67520-5
1. English language—Alphabet—Juvenile literature.
2. Animals—Juvenile literature.   [1. Alphabet.   2. Animals.
3. English language—Verb.]   I. Title.
PE1155.B395   1996   421'.1—dc20   [E]
94-37189   CIP   AC

Published in the United States by Lodestar Books,
an affiliate of Dutton Children's Books,
a division of Penguin Books USA Inc.,
375 Hudson Street,
New York, New York 10014

Published simultaneously in Canada
by McClelland & Stewart, Toronto

Editor: Rosemary Brosnan   Designer: Marilyn Granald

Printed in Hong Kong   First Edition
10 9 8 7 6 5 4 3 2 1

Dedicated to

KAREN, CRAIG, and LAWRENCE,

with much love . . .

and with special thanks to TERESA BENZWIE, whose book,
A Moving Experience (Zephyr Press), inspired this book

Ants anchor **Aa**

Bats boil **Bb**

Cows carry Cc

Dodos decorate Dd

Elephants embrace **Ee**

Frogs follow Ff

Goats guard Gg

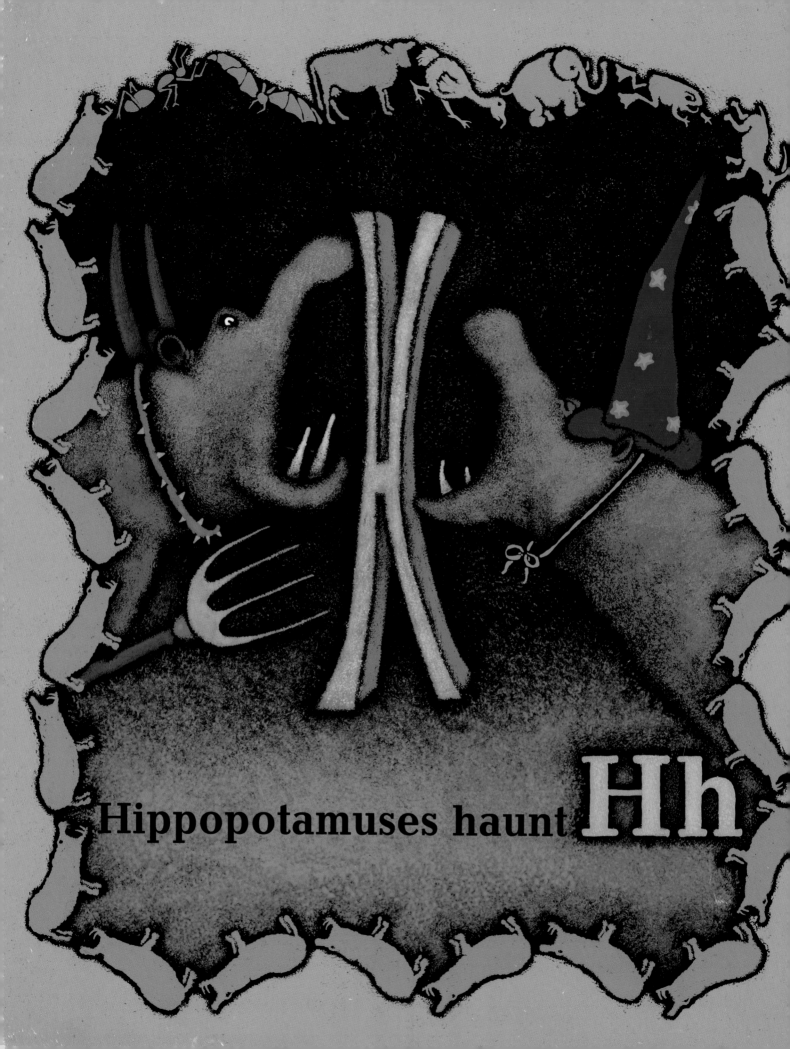

Hippopotamuses haunt Hh

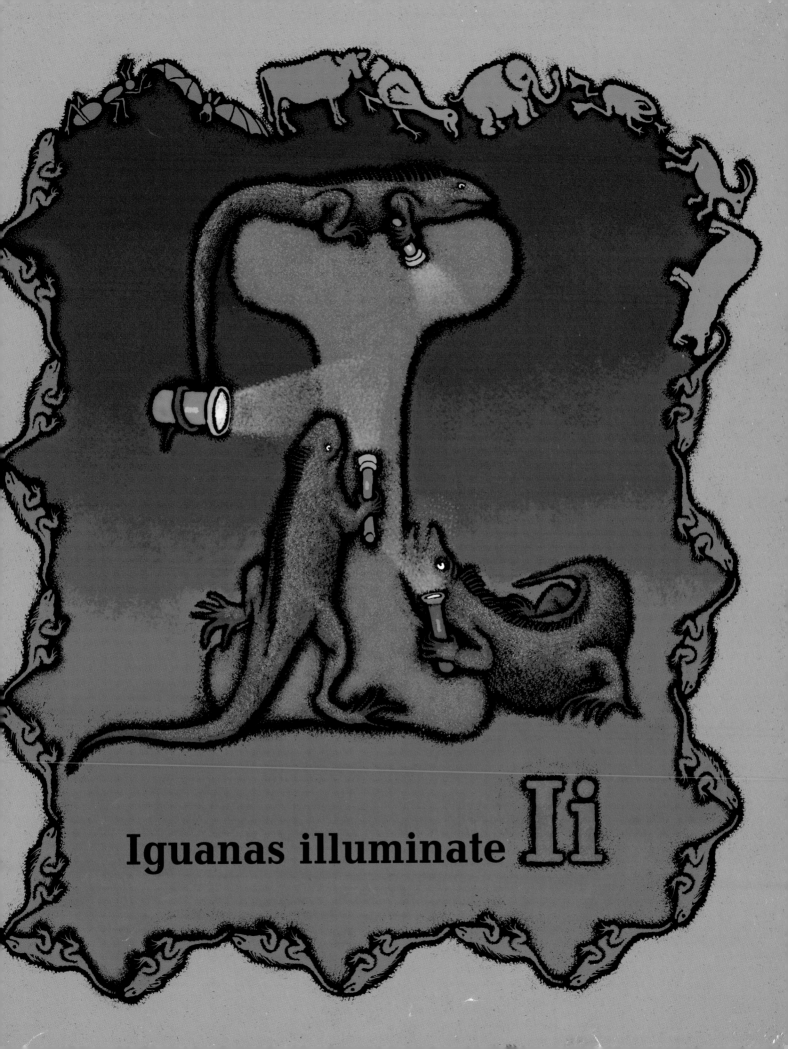

Iguanas illuminate Ii

Jaguars jostle **Jj**

Kangaroos kiss **Kk**

Lions launch Ll

Mice mail **Mm**

Narwhals needle **Nn**

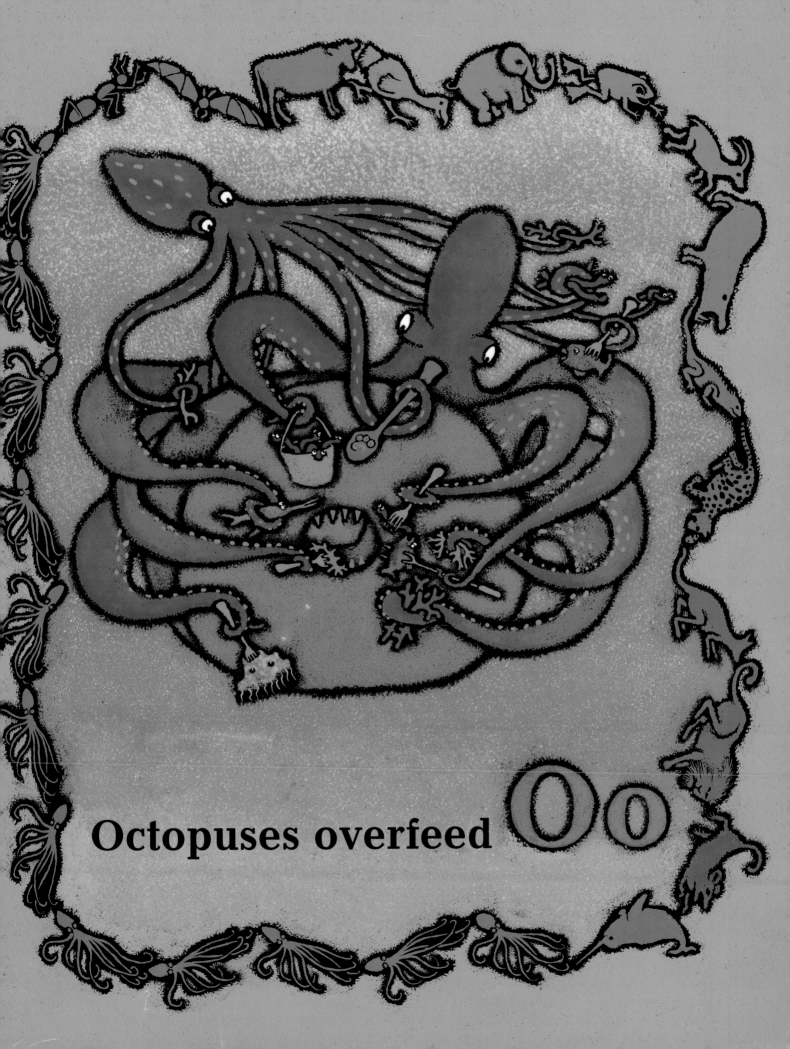

Octopuses overfeed Oo

Pigs purchase **Pp**

Quails quilt Qq

Rhinoceroses ruin Rr

Snakes saw Ss

Turtles tackle **Tt**

Unicorns undress **Uu**

Voles visit Vv

Walruses wrestle **Ww**

Xanthid crabs x-ray **Xx**

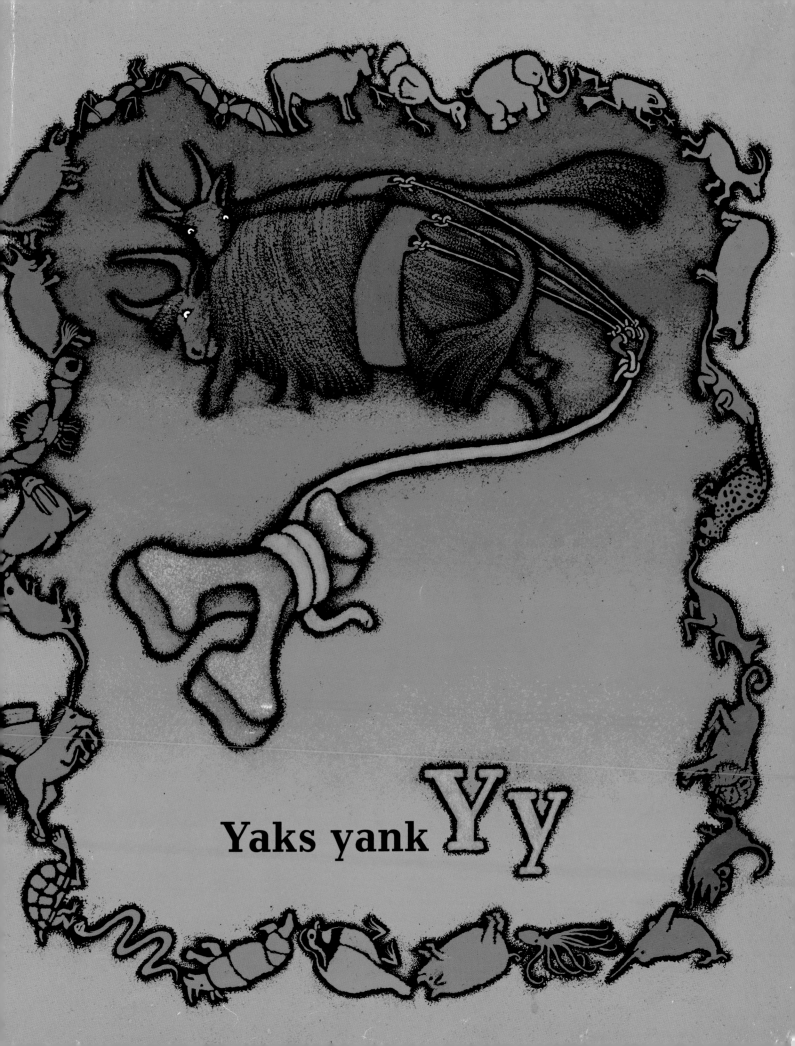

Yaks yank Yy

Zebras zipper Zz